# History of the Development of United States Tanks, Including Current Plans and Trends (Tank Course 1937-1938)

## G. A. Hadsell

THE INFANTRY SCHOOL
Fort Benning, Georgia

TANK COURSE
1937-1938

HISTORY OF THE DEVELOPMENT OF UNITED STATES TANKS, INCLUDING

CURRENT PLANS AND TRENDS

Captain G. A. Hadsell, Infantry.

# TABLE OF CONTENTS Page

## BIBLIOGRAPHY                                    Abbreviations

Fighting Tanks        Particularly usefull in this     F.T. since 1916
Since 1916-Icks       study. Excellent summary of
                      combat histories

Army Ordnance         Icks article in May-June'37      A.O.
                      Very useful summary.

Military and          Usefull for background only      not cited
Naval Digest
~what ones~

Tank Development      Very good reference for early    Brett
File, Major Brett.    stages of tank development and   World
                      War battle experience.

Tank Characteristics, An essential paper in            Howie
Development           preparation of this
and Design-Howie      study

Field Service Regulations For principles Tank          F.S.R. 1923
1923                      Employment.

Command and General   Excellent for background         not cited
Staff School Quarterly and foreign trends.
~what ones~

Infantry Journal      Very useful in providing         "   "
~what ones~           background.

Various Histories,    Used for sketches and to         Sketches copied only
Dictionaries and      refresh memory on general
Encyclopedias         history.

Lecture Notes         Medium Tank data, digested       not cited
Captain Black         for use

Aberdeen Proving Ground The authority on               A.P.G. ENG. DATA .
Engineering Data        technical data.

Infantry School Pamphlet: Tank tactics.               I.S.'37-'38 G.P.T.E.

Note:    No list has been made of the tracings, copies or sketches
         appearing in the text since they have no purpose other than
         to be suggestive.  They are not intended to be accurately
         descriptive.

*Bibliography not sufficiently detailed for actual use.*
*Is only a vague guide. ~F.*

"Plus ça change, plus c'est la même chose."

## INTRODUCTION

"The appearance of the motor on the battlefield gives mobility its former significance" says the French General Buat. "Mechanized armies have brought back the mobility of Genghis Khan, Tamerlane and Alexander", asserts a British writer. Another authority claims that the next war may begin in the air but it will end as always in the mud. Which statement will History more nearly justify?

Do we need swarms of light tanks to imitate the Tartar hordes? Must we have harder hitting vehicles for sledge hammer blows against strong prepared positions? Will large armies venture into the open without the protection of air craft and tank masses? What is the role of obstacles in the new-old combat of today and to-morrow? Will cities become focal points for savage defense as in medieval Europe and modern Spain?

Shall we slow down our tanks to the advance of foot troops? Shall we speed up some of the Infantry to rush in with grenades, sub-machine guns and other automatic weapons in the wake of fast tanks? Are tanks to be used only at the critical moment of battle? Shall we organize armored or mechanized divisions to strike swiftly at flanks or communications? Would such forces, moving on interior lines become vital factors in protecting our thousands of miles of border and coast?

Will anti-tank guns rout our mechanized power as the long bow destroyed French Chivalry at Crecy? What of foot troops destroying tanks with bombs and bottles of gasolene? What effect have headlines from Guadalajara, Shanghai and Teruel on present plans and trends?

Are tanks Infantry or Cavalry? Are they either? Do they partake of the traditional functions of both upon occasion? If Napoleon and other great leaders of bygone days knew how to combine all degrees of mobility on the battlefield, can we learn from their classic battle plans? Or is all this so new that there is nothing to be learned from the past?

What are the desirable characteristics of a fighting tank? Are our tanks too fast? Are there occasions when speed will become the most important factor? Do they carry enough armor? Too much armor? Do they have sufficient fire power? How effective is fire from a moving tank? Do we need different types of tanks for different types of missions?

Now, of course, it is much easier to ask than to answer. But by asking we may perhaps begin to chart the extent of our ignorance and outline the boundaries of the terrain we should like eventually to explore. Certainly we should not expect to cover much of the field in this preliminary study. We can, however, try to get at some of the ideas and some of the facts which have influenced tank development in the United States. We may attempt to analyze current plans and trends. And finally we may try to reason to a certain number of conclusions. But in the end we shall still have many more questions than answers. And our answers must be progressively modified as we may be permitted further study and experience.

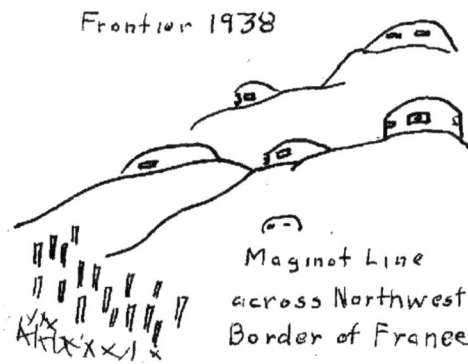

Frontier 1938

Maginot Line
across Northwest
Border of France

Mass, Mobility Shock Action

## GENERAL IDEAS

"Tanks are mechanically propelled, armored vehicles, combining the powers of fire and movement"(1). Again, "The tank is a combat vehicle, its principle characteristics being: a combination of fire power, mobility, protection, shock action"(2). And again, "A tank is a self-propelled vehicle of the track-laying type, combining fire power, mobility, protection and shock action"(3). Its mission is to carry "protected fire power and shock action into the enemy position"(4).

In these definitions the most spectacular thing is not, perhaps, that tanks combine mobility, fire power, protection and shock action, but that these characteristics are combined in a mechanically-propelled, land vehicle. During the quarter of a million years that we humans have been bickering here below, mobility and shock action in land warfare have depended upon the live leg power of elephant, bullock, horse, or man himself. And now the internal combustion engine is to furnish some of the push.

Many still view this innovation with no little skepticism. But the historian may instead wonder why it took the Machine Age so long to produce a land war ship. Hundreds of thousands have trusted their lives

(1) F.S.R. 1923. (2) Howie. (3) F.T. since 1916. (4) I.S.'37-'38 G.P.T.E.

to mechanically propelled craft on the sea and in the air. And on land
the development of civilian motor transportation has been phenominal.
Unfortunately, the cross-country requirements of military vehicles gave
rise to special problems. But these problems have largely been solved
and the tank is ready to take its place among other self-propelled weapons;
among them, the naval "battle wagon" and the more spectacular air ship.
Certainly if machines can fight on the sea and in the air they will do as
well or better on good terra-firma.

Since it is now a sure thing that fast, mechanically reliable tanks
can be produced, attention has shifted back to tactical considerations.
Fast, reliable tanks are being turned out in some quantity in this
country. Experience in their use has been accumulated and their characteristics
of fire power, mobility and shock action and protection are being evaluated.
At the same time these characteristics are being subjected to minute
examination to determine what modifications in existing types may be
desirable. In other words, today, in 1938, military men in the United
States are asking and answering the questions: "What types of tanks are
most needed? How many and what types of guns? How much armor?
How much speed?"

?

# CHAPTER I

## HISTORICAL RETROSPECT

Compared to Britain's long experience in peace and war, France's mechanized thousands, Russia's reputed tank hordes, Germany's phenominal and recent expansion, our progress along these lines may seem less impressive. However, although we may appear to have less to show for our efforts, we have been very thorough. Actually we have produced no less than 37[*] different models of tanks. And fortunately we have not gone into quantity production on any of the intervening types. Thus we probably have fewer obsolete or obsolescent types in service than other great nations. Hence it begins to look as if our slow start may have been an advantage after all. *However it is here that we have finally started. But*

We shall not try to trace our tank development in any great detail. Instead, this brief study will be devided into three parts, namely:

1. World War Types.

2. Experimental Types.

3. Christie Types.

This division is rather artificial since the first Christie was produced in 1919 (5) and our present Medium Tank might be considered as as a Christie type. The Christies, however, have exerted an important influence on our tank development and doctrine and hence appear to warrant a grouping to themselves. Actually, also, all our tanks have been experimental in the sense that they have been progressively modified or improved. Present type tanks will be considered in another chapter. Certain models will not be mentioned here at all and others will be treated in an order other than that of their production. In an effort to partly supply this deficiency a chronological table has been placed at the end of this paper.

---

[*]For an explanation of how this figure was obtained, see chronological table at the end of this paper.

(5) F.T. since 1916.

WORLD WAR TYPES (6)

Before we go to experimental types, we should perhaps dwell for
a moment on the tanks which our soldiers saw in the World War. All
our veteran tankers have served with these types and practically all
those senior officers who guide our destinies saw these tanks in battle
either in the hands of the French or British or in our American Tank
Corps. Experience with these fighting tanks therefore forms an essential
part of the background in the history of our tank development.

---

THE FRENCH RENAULT TYPE TANK

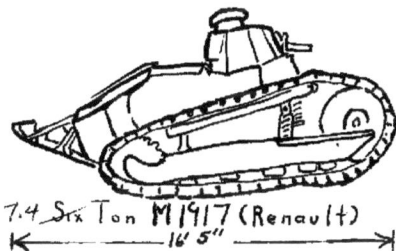

7.4 Six Ton M1917 (Renault)
16' 5"

This tough little two man tank is interesting for several reasons.
A Renault sits beside our School near the big British"Heavy", looking
for all the world like a pigmy among giants. Even our new M-2, rated
as a light tank, seems a monster of bulk beside it. Yet the sturdy
little Renault, for all its faults, helped many thousands of doughboys
to advance over some of the most difficult battlefields of the World
War. The Renault was highly efficient in cleaning out machine gun nests
and never hesitated to take after anything in its path,- even German
field batteries.

It is interesting because, even more than the British "heavy", it
was rated as an Infantry Accompanying tank. That is;- it usually
assisted "by close and continuous cooperation infantry battalions in
the attack." And this question of Accompanying Tanks  has never

---

(6) The matter in this section is practically all drawn from F.T. since 1916
Some matter also came from Major Brett's photostat file on Tank
Development. Matter also from Conf.

ceased to be absorbing. Furthermore, although the French used some
heavier tanks, the Renault was probably the type seen most often by
veterans of the A.E.F. It was the tank which most often assisted
our American assault waves forward, and it was the weapon of our
344th and 345th American Tank Battalions in the St. Mihiel offensive
and the inferno of the Meuse-Argonne. Even after the war it was
probably our best known tank since we had 952 of them , produced in
1918 and 1919.

Although the wartime Renault is now as extinct as the Dodo, it
did possess many qualities still considered interesting or desirable.
For example, due to its queer looking tail, its trench crossing ability
of 7 feet comapares well with many bigger tanks. Also, from the front
it presented a very small target. And in view of the discussion which
sometimes arises when two or three are gathered together, it is interesting
to note that it had a revolving turret and not a fixed gun mount. It
may be interesting too that many Renaults mounted a 37 mm. gun instead
of a machine gun. Probably as important as anything else was the
advantageous position of the driver in front where he could see, the
gunner in the center and the engine out of the way of the crew in the
rear of the tank.

The worst that could be said of the Renault,-and this is probably
sufficiently damning,- was that it was underpowered (only 5.8 horse
power per ton), that it was slow, and that it had many mechanical
troubles. The best, is probably that it has seen service in many lands
and that, as modernized, it is in some countries still a popular type.
As the first light tank to accumulate considerable battlefield experience,
it may also be said to symbolize a school of thought when its merits or
deficiencies may be compared to heavier types. That such a sturdy, simple
tank might be produced at comparatively low cost in very large quantities
is at least thought provoking.

## THE MARK VIII TANK

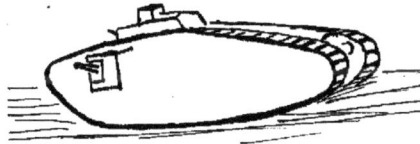

Mark VIII, 43.5 Tons

← 34' 2¼" →

This tank, of British inspiration, was not produced by our Ordnance Department until after the war in 1919 when 100 were built. It is, however, generally similar to the heavy British tanks whose massed waves smashed for miles though German defenses at Cambrai and Amiens. It is like the big Mark V Star which stands beside our School and belonged to the 301st American Tank Battalion, which with British and American doughboys broke the Hindenburg Line.

Tanks of this type owed their remarkable success in battle to their huge bulk and crushing power; to the fire power of their heavy battery of guns,- six pounders (2.24 inches) and from four to seven machine guns; to their remarkable obstacle ability; and to the fact that they were manned by picked crews of the toughest fighting men the world has ever seen.

Toward the end of the war 1914-1918 these tanks attacked in mass and in successive waves, over 400 being used in a single battle on a relatively narrow front. Although some outfits suffered 70% casualties in tanks, the advance nevertheless went on through barbed wire, over deep trenches, in the face of machine gun and anti-tank gun fire, through enemy 77 mm. artillery firing at point blank range.

Examples are on record of these slow, 4 mile per hour leviathans chugging into the midst of German "sacrifice" field batteries, killing the crews, silencing the guns. In one action one tank company crushed

170 machine guns.(7)  An instance of their obstacle ability was the crossing of the dry Canal du Nord in the Second Battle of Cambrai. The Germans had cut away the banks to provide a nine foot vertical drop, the dry canal being 50 feet wide, 12 feet deep and under enemy fire.

These big tanks _led_ the infantry, _supported_ the infantry and cavalry, and were themselves supposted by all arms.  They cooperated with lighter whippet tanks, with armored cars, and upon occasion even at that early date used radio communication successfully.  At times they carried machine gun squads forward in their foul, fume filled bellies-- though it is recorded that often the infantry to be carried forward preferred to take their chances outside. (7)     All in all, a reading and re-reading of the combat histories of the"Heavies" is an inspiration to the student, and like the combat history of the Renaults is packed with food for thought.

------

While we are not particularly concerned here with exact dimensions, the general contours of the Mark VIII are perhaps interesting.  Although the big tanks were over 34 feet long, they were only about 8 feet high and about 12 feet wide. (8)  The length gave great obstacle ability ( 16 foot trench), yet from the front these tanks did not offer a much greater target than some modern tanks.  Its shape, with its sponsons (and this point becomes interesting when we begin to think about the proposed T 5),  also made it capable of mounting a much greater battery of guns than is usual nowadays.  Taken all together, the Mark VIII was a remarkably compact fighting unit.  Another interesting feature was an intra-tank telephone.

Today the weaknesses of this type are more stressed than its powers. And this is no more than reasonable, since it was slow, ponderous, and likely to break down mechanically.  Its armor, also, was comparatively _(what thickness?)_ light.  But again, combat records appear to show that its accomplishments under fire were remarkable.  Hence if obstacles ever again threaten to play a major role in warfare, there may be features of the big tank which will warrant further study.  The big tank also, therefore, may be said to symbolize a certain line of thought.

(7) F.T. since 1916.     (8) Howie.

### EXPERIMENTAL TYPES (9)

We shall not here concern ourselves with the flame throwing, steam tank produced in 1918, nor with a unique looking skeleton tank which proposed to combine lightness with obstacle ability, nor can we devote space to many other interesting experimental models. We can only try to trace the main features of tank development from the war toward the present.

MEDIUM TANKS

Medium T 1, 22 Tons
21' 6"

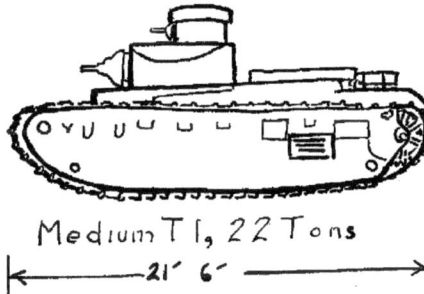

In view of the decided reawakening of interest in 1937 and 1938 in heavier tanks it may be worth our while to consider three tanks produced between 1921 and 1925. These; the Medium A, Model 1921, the Medium, Model 1922 and the Medium T 1 (1925); weighed between 22 and 25 tons and attained a speed of between 10 and 15 miles per hour. The maximum armor thickness was one inch. Since present tanks use aircraft engines, we might mention that two of these used marine engines in an attempt to find sufficient power.

Interesting features of these mediums were their turrets, the upper of which was revolving, their comparatively heavy armament of one 2.24 inch cannon and two caliber .30 machine guns, and the positions of the crew of four with the driver in front and the gunners in the center.

(9) F.T. since 1916 and Howie.

The engine was in rear. We may note also, that even in these heavy vehicles, speed is already twice or three times that of wartime types. On the opposite side of the ledger, we find lack of power and the fact that considerable progress needed to be made in track and suspension systems. Soon, also, we find a definite trend in the cycle of development toward lighter types.

In spite of faults, however, the last of these, the Medium T 1, was considered to be "fairly well suited to a definite tactical mission- that of the leading role." That is,- it could be used "to break the way in mass for a main effort against a hostile flank or for the main effort of a penetration." (10) This, we may remember, is reminiscent of the system evolved by the British during the war. However, none of the Mediums produced during this period appeared sufficiently suitable to be produced in quantity;- although, much later, the Medium T 1 was modified by the installation of a Liberty V-12 engine and called the Medium T 1-E 1.(11)

## Medium T2, 15 Tons

The Medium T 2, though produced as late as 1930, is in a sense a link between the past and the future. It is lighter than the mediums just considered and is capable of a speed of between 20 and 25 miles per hour. Some of its characteristics show the influence

(10) F.T. since 1916.

(11) Howie.

of the Light T 1 series, begun in 1927. It is linked to older types by
its weight and by its considerable battery of guns, -one 1.85 cannon and
one 37 mm. gun, one caliber .30 machine gun, one caliber .50 machine gun.
By its weight and its armament it may also be considered to be linked to
the new proposed T 5. Mechanically, it undoubtedly represented a considerable
advance over older tanks, although the arrangement of the gunners'
compartment was inconvenient and the position of the engine in front was
undesirable. ( 12)

## THE T 1 SERIES OF LIGHT TANKS

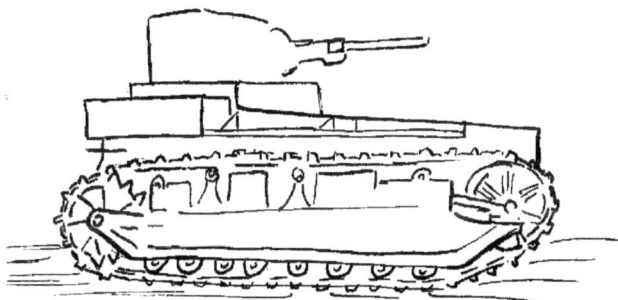

Light Tank T1-E3

    The first of these, the Light Tank, T 1, came out in 1927. It marks
a definite trend in the production of fast, light tanks, though the T 1
itself was considerably slower than present models. It may also be said
to mark a definite milestone in military thought, just as the lessons of
the present Spanish War may be said to mark another. For it was about
this time that the possibility of using mechanized or armored forces
began to be given very serious consideration. (13)   This meant, of course,
a feeling that obstacles and fortified positions were to play a lesser
role than in 1914-1918. Moreover, the fact that one of these tanks (14)

(12) F.T. since 1916.
  (13) A. O. May-June 1928, Major L.H. Campbell,Jr-"Automotive Equipment of Armies".
  (14) A. O. March-April 1929, Maj. Gen. C.C. Williams- "Mechanization".

had completed "2000 miles at high speed without major overhaul" was
vastly exciting to military minds and appeared to open new and fascinating
vistas for the future of armies.

Obviously, these little tanks were mechanically an enormous
improvement over previous models and a far cry from the Great War when
mechanical troubles alone might have immobilized an entire tank
platoon. However, the models from T 1 to T 1-E 3 had the engine in
front, as did also the T 1-E 5. This condition was hard on the using
personnel. In the T 1-E 4, and T 1-E 6, however, this condition was
corrected and the engine was put at the rear where it belonged.(15)

Light Tank T1-E4

To get some idea*of how this T 1 series unfolded we might mention
that the T 1 Light Tank was followed by the T 1-E 1, of which 4 were
built. Then in 1929 the T 1-E 2 appeared. Now to go back to the four
T 1-E 1's, we find one of these modified and called the T 1-E 3. Then,
very likely influenced in some degree by the tests of the British
Vickers-Armstrong which were very satisfactory, another of the original
T 1-E 1's was given an improved suspension system and given a reversed
arrangement of driving, fighting compartment and engine. This was
called the T 1-E 4. In 1932, also, another of the four was given the
Cleveland Tractor Company 's controlled differential steering unit in
place of the old clutch brake type. This was a big step toward the M-2,-
and this light tank was called the T 1-E 5. Still another of the T 1-E 1 ' s

*An idea only, since while we can quote eminent authority we are not entirely
sure of having read aright.
(15) A.P.G. Eng. Data.

or rather the T 1-E 1 which had already become the T 1-E 4, was further modified to incorporate the 244 horse power, American La France V-12 engine. This was called the Light Tank T 1-E 6 and closes the T 1 series. (16) (17)

In general, tanks of this series weighed between 7 and almost 10 tons, their maximum armor plate was 5/8 inches thick, their speed was in the neighborhood of 20 miles per hour. The horse/was, in general, power per ton close to 18. They carried one 37 mm gun and one caliber .30 machine gun in a revolving turret. (17)

Before leaving these light tanks we can do no better than to quote from Mr. Robert J Icks: "The stamina shown by the T 1 light tank series gave an indication that it might be possible to eliminate trucks as tank carriers with a resultant simplification of organization and supply. Since then, the goal has been to eliminate the use of trucks and to develop light tanks which are possessed of sufficient stamina and speed to possess their own strategical mobility. The Christie tanks first proved that this effect might be achieved."(18). In addition to mechanical reliability, we thus see another important cleavage between the old and the new- strategical mobility. And here is where many believed they saw a reconquest of the mobility of Ghengis Khan, Tamerlane, and Alexander- to say nothing of Napolen.

———————

(16) A.P.G. Eng. Data.

(17) Howie.

(18) A. O. May-June 1937, Robert J. Icks, Captain 423rd Infantry (Light Tanks),-Page 332. "Four Decades of Mechanization".

## CHRISTIE TYPES

Medium Tank

Christie T-3
Weight 10½ Tons

That a former racing driver(19) should have become a designer of tanks may be interesting for two reasons. As civilians are only too glad to admit for us, and as some military men will acknowledge, we soldiers, some of us anyhow, appear inclined to conservatism and prone to trust past experience rather to the exclusion of theory. Thus, as some would have it, we perhaps need a periodic bombshell to align us with the times. If this is so, such a bombshell may well have been provided by the performance of the 1928 Christies.

"So extraordinary were the results achieved in the first tests in October, 1928, that not only did mechanization enthusiasts in this country advocate immediate adoption of this tank, but representatives of other nations made arrangements for purchase as well."(20) The other reason is that this former racing driver, Mr. J. Walter Christie was naturally interested in speed, and still more speed!

With the two Christies produced before 1928 we are not particularly concerned. But the 1928 and 1931 Christies introduced a new type of suspension and a new high in performance and speed. Those whose

(19) Conf.

(20) A. O. May-June 1937, Icks. P. 338. "Four Decades of Mechanization"

imaginations had been stirred by visions of tank hordes swooping down "like the wolf on the fold" may easily have believed that their dreams had come true. For the 1931 Christie (T 3) would do over 40 miles an hour across country and with the track removed on the road, 70 miles per hour! Here was mobility with a vengeance. With the Christies also, tankers began to hope for their first truly modern fighting machines since the war. And this was important, too, since the wartime Renaults and Mark VIII's were just about due for retirement after long and faithful service.

Three of these Christies were delivered to the Infantry and called, Convertible Medium Tank, T 3. Their remarkable reserve power was indicated by their high horse power per ton of 32.2, the highest in any tank to date(21). Armor was from .25 to .625/and the armement inches was one 37 mm. gun and one caliber .30 machine gun. The wheel type suspension was comparatively durable and gave an excellent base or gun platform from which to use the weapons. This last item may be summarized in the expression, "excellent riding qualities", for which Christie Types are justly famous. With these three tanks, which have in their turn become obsolete, we close our brief historical summary. The T 3's now repose as decorations for the left front of the Tank School and the entrances to the Tank Parks here at Benning.

T3E1 ?

(21) Conf.

# CHAPTER II

## PRESENT TYPES

# Medium Tank T3E2
### Weight    14.1 Tons
### Width      8′
### Height    7′8″

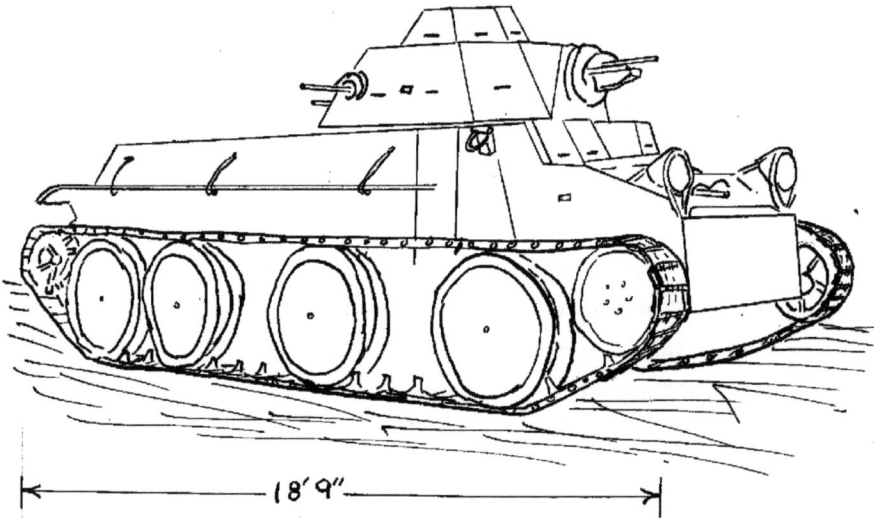

|← 18′9″ →|

Having just finished off three medium Christies, now gone
to discard, we can conveniently carry on with five more Christie type
tanks. These are close to obsolescence but still on the rolls.
At present, the T3-E 2 is chiefly interesting because it may afford
comparison with the proposed T-5 (22). Not that the two types may be
similar in many respects, but possibly because certain features of the
T-5 superstructure may recall the earlier tank. The armament of the
T 3-E 2,though less powerful than that of the new tank, also suggests
the trend. (See sketch on this page and on page 7?.)

(22) Conf.

The T 3-E 2 is interesting because it is the first type, considered here, to be powered with an air craft engine. This was the D-12 Curtis water cooled unit, developing 435 brake horse power. (23)   The use of an air craft engine, though possibly not the final step, represents a long stride in the search for adequate, light power.   Speed of this tank was 35 miles per hour on tracks and 57.6 on wheels. (23)  The heavy armament has already been noted. This consisted of one 37 mm. gun and four caliber .30 machine guns.

We shall not tarry longer here than to suggest again that the Medium T 3-E 2 may be another link in the chain toward heavier and more powerful tanks.  The T 3-E 2 was considered by some authorities to have been an excellent tank (24).  And while it too, may be close to the scrap heap, some of its features may live on in the new T 5. Our latest information is that four of the T 3-E 2's may furnish replacement parts for a fifth which will run comparative tests with the T-5. (25).

----------

MEDIUM TANK T 4

The tank outlined on the opposite page  is, except for the turret and several minor details, similar to the present armament of Company "F", 67th Infantry.  This organization has now 15 of the T 4's and 3 of the T 4-E 1's, which last differ only in having a barbette superstructure.  In these  tanks improvements over previous types have continued.  The T 4 has now the controlled differential steering found so desirable in the T 1-E 5.   The engine is the same Continental Radial Aircraft unit which we shall find in the M 2.  While the speed has been rated as high as 70 miles per hour on wheels and 45 on tracks, it may be that 35 mph across country is closer to the normal maximum.

While from some points of view the T 4 may appear underpowered, its users are very loyal to it.   They like its steady gun platform and the easy riding afforded by the Christie type suspension.

(23) Conf.
)24) A.P.G. Eng. Data.
(25) Conf. Hereafter, unless other wise noted, authority for any
    statements made in the body of the text may be assumed to the
    results of conferences with members of this command. The student,
    however, hastens to absolve these generous individuals from all
    responsibility for any errors which may appear therein, since he
    realizes only too well the inadequacy of his memory.

*? always rather*

However, there may be at times apparent a certain lack of elbow room
inside. This, of course, is to be expected, although in comparison
with the M 2, the interior of the T 4 seems less roomy than might be
expected from the exterior dimensions. In any case, the T 4 has not
been recommended for standardization and it may be expected that the
T 5 will take its place.  *Height well have included the reason for lack of room compared with over all width = convertible feature*

## THE M 2 TANK ( 26 )

*However it would have been well to do so as done for previous other types mentioned*

The student would scarcely be expected to make extensive comment
where detailed information is so readily available. Hence we shall
merely pause to show where the development considered up to now leads
with the M 2. We remember that the T 1 series closed with the attainment
of a very satisfactory light tank, and that one of the greatest
achievements was the adoption of the controlled differential type of
steering.

In the T 2, which was the next step (1933), the controlled differential
steering was retained as well as the spring and bogie suspension of the
T 1-E 6. The big advance was the installation of the Continental radial
aircraft engine which doubled the available power, giving the high speed
of 45 miles per hour. After tests in 1934, the volute spring suspension
was substituted for the British Vickers-Armstrong type and found to
give greater satisfaction(27). The tank was then called the T 2-E 1
and when later recommended for standardization, the M 2 A 1. This
type had a single turret. Another M 2 with two turrets was called the
M 2 A 2. Still another type with guns mounted in <u>barbette</u>,- that is, no
turrets- was called the M2-A 3. *error* In the meantime, a rubber block track
had been installed, which afforded the necessary strategical mobility
over pavement.  *Confused with CGTS*

With the distribution of 282 of these tanks to the Infantry, the
dream of many a veteran tanker would seem close to realization. Here,
at last he has a powerful, fast, mechanically reliable fighting machine.
And now at long last the necessary experience with modern tanks in quantity
can be obtained.

(26) T-41 M
(27) Howie.

## CHAPTER III

### CURRENT PLANS AND TRENDS

### THE T 5

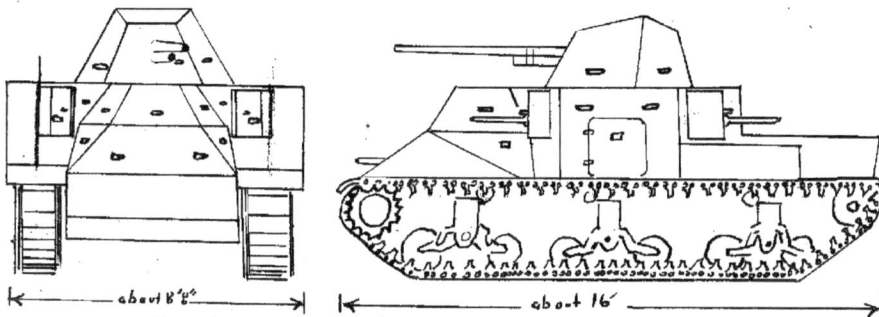

An attempt to Visualize the Appearance
of the
**Proposed T5 Tank**
Weight about 18 Tons

about 8'2"     about 16'

The sketch above, while by no means to scale, is inspired by the blue print of the Pilot Model Medium Tank T-5. Understanding that the suspension system would be that of the M 2 with an additional set of wheels, we have tried to draw the track and suspension system not shown on the blue print. The result is a loss of perspective somewhere. However it will perhaps provide a general idea.

It is probable that two such tanks will be furnished for test, one with an engine developing in the neighborhood of 400 horsepower the other to be the same as in the M 2 Tank. The speed will be determined by test but will undoubtedly be considerably less than that of the M 2. Armor will probably reach a maximum of 1 5/8 inches. The fire power will be furnished by a cannon which may be 1.85 inches or else a new and improved 37mm. As already mentioned, the T-5 wil probably be tested in comparison with the T 3-E 2.

### HEAVIER ARMOR PLATE ON M 2

Another current project is an increase of the M 2 armor to a maximum

of one inch in front of the driver and bow gun, with proportionate
increases in other plates. ~~~~ ~~~~~~

## Diesel Engines

Due to the desire to reduce fire hazards in tanks and to provide
maximum torque at low speeds ,considerable experimentation with Diesels
is being carried on. The possibility of tanks being set on fire by
containers of gasolene thrown over them by the enemy has sharpened the
activity in this field. Maintenance difficulties here bar progress.

## CHAPTER IV

## PRESENT TRENDS

In the United States, having no war close at hand to furnish'
actual battle experience, and having fewer tanks to experiment with,
we are necessarily much influenced by European trends. These may
be summarized as a much more extensive use of tank obstacles than
was believed possible a few years ago, a phenominal development
in the efficiency of anti-tank guns, a lesser use of mobility than
was believed advisable in recent years. Hence there is a decided
trend in the development of heavier tanks, thicker armor, more
powerful armement. Light tanks of the type used in Spain have been
partially discredited, though this would not seem to apply to our M 2
since it is of much sturdier construction and fire power.

As for the question of revolving turret vs barbette type mounts,
this appears to have resolved itself into a sort of compromise , wherein
turrets are used for the main battery and fixed mounts for machine guns.
A further compromise may be indicated in the use of sponson mounts in
the T 5. The main objections to turrets, that they may jam and are hard
to operate when the tank is moving, are perhaps not impossible of solution.
At any rate, small tanks mounting only one or two guns appear likely to
retain the turret. Larger Tanks seem likely to combine turret and
barbette mounts.

CHRONOLOGICAL LIST OF U.S. TANKS.

DATA TAKEN LARGELY FROM HOWIE

THOUGH REFERENCE WAS MADE ALSO

TO F.T. since 1916 and A.P.G

Eng. Data.

(This list to accompany Monograph 1937-1938, "HISTORY OF
THE DEVELOPMENT OF U.S. TANKS." G.A. HADSELL, Capt. Inf.)

Name:    Gas Electric - 1918   ( 1 built )

Crew:    6

General Arrangements:    Driver and Howitzer in front, driver above engine in rear.

Weight:    25 Tons

Dimensions:    Length 16 ft. 6 in.    Width 9 ft. 1 in.
Height 7 ft 9½ in.

Clearance:

Fording:

Armament:    1-75 mm (2.95 in) Mountain Howitzer and 2 cal. .30 machine guns

Armor:    0.25 in. to 0.63 in.

Engine:    One Holt - 4 cyl. 90 HP. with Electric Generator and an electric motor for each track.

Speed:    6 M. P. H.

Transmission:    Electric

Steering:    By the varying current to driving motors and by braking.

Cruising Radius:

Slope Climbing:

Suspension:    Coil springs, Rollers and Bogies.

Tracks:    Flat steel plates with double grousers. Pitch 7½ in.
Width 15½ in.

Obstacle Ability:

Spanning:

Ground Pressure:

Remarks:    This was the first tank built in the United States.

## CHARACTERISTICS, U. S. TANKS

Name:              Steam Tank. -Track Laying. 1918 ( 1 built )

Crew:              8

General Arrangements:   Driver and Flame Thrower in front;  Water and
                   Kerosene tanks in center;  2 mgs. in one sponson on
                   each side;  Boilers and Engines in rear.

Weight:            50 Tons.

Dimensions:        Length- 34 ft. 9 in.   Width- 12 ft. 6 in.  Height 10 ft
                   4½ in.

Clearance:

Fording:

Armament:          One flame thrower and four Cal. .30 MGS.

Armor:             0.5 in.

Engine:            2 cylinder steam engine, one for each track and one kerosene
                   burner for each engine.  Total HP- 500.

Speed:             4 MPH.

Transmission:      Sliding gears,  2 speeds forward and 1 reverse.
                   Large exposed gears and shafts in rear part of hull

Steering:

Cruising Radius:

Slope Climbing:

Suspension:        Rigid with three rollers.

Tracks:            Flat steel plates with grousers, width 24 in, pitch 12½ in.-
                   upper part of track supported by three rollers.

Obstacle Ability:

Spanning:

Ground Pressure:

Remarks:           Produced by the Corps of Engineers U.S. A.   This was the
                   second tank built in the U.S.

# CHARACTERISTICS, U. S. TANKS

Name:                 Steam Tank. —# wheeled 1918 ( 1 built )

Crew:                 6

General Arrangements:   Howitzer and gunner low in front, driver above, engines in center, Machine Guns above engines, boilers and tanks in rear.

Weight:               17 Tons

Dimensions:          Length–22 ft. 3 in. Height– 9 ft. 10 in. Width– 10 ft. 1 in.

Clearance:

Fording:

Armament:            1 –75 mm. Mountain Howitzer and two Cal. .30 MGS.

Armor:                0.25 in to 0.63 in.

Engine:               2 double 2 cylinder steam engines– combined HP–150.

Speed:                5 MPH.    8.8 HP per Ton.

Transmission:

Steering:

Cruising Radius:

Slope Climbing:

Suspension:          Rigid (on wheels)    Tracks –none.

Tracks:               None

Obstacle Ability:

Spanning:

Ground Pressure:

Remarks:            Produced by Holt Tractor Company 1918.

# CHARACTERISTICS, U. S. TANKS

Name:        Skeleton Tank 1918  ( 1 built )

Crew:     2

General Arrangements: Driver in front, gunner in turret in rear; at each side
                      from front to rear, radiator, engine and transmission.

Weight:        8 Tons

Dimensions:        Length- 25 ft.  Width 8 ft. 5 in. Height- 9 ft. 6 in.

Clearance:

Fording:

Armament:        1 Cal. .30 MG

Armor:        0.5 in.

Engine:        2 Beaver 4 cylinder.   Combined HP- 100.

Speed:        5 MPH.   12.5 HP per Ton.

Transmission:        2 speeds forward, 1 reverse.

Steering:

Cruising Radius:

Slope Climbing:

Suspension:        Rigid, with rollers.

Tracks:        Width 12 in.  Pitch 11 in.

Obstacle Ability:

Spanning:

Ground Pressure:

Remarks:        Built with a view of securing a light weight vehicle, capable
                of crossing wide trenches.  Many structural members were pieces
                of iron pipe, with standard plumbing connections.  Produced by
                Pioneer Tractor Company.

-4-

## CHARACTERISTICS, U. S. TANKS

Name:         Ford- 3 Ton 1918 ( 15 built )

Crew:         2

General Arrangements: Driver and gunner in front, driver on right, engines and final drive in rear.

Weight:       3.1 Tons

Dimensions:   Length-13 ft. 8 in.  Width -5 ft. 8 in.  Height 5 ft 3 in.

Clearance:

Fording:      21 inches.

Armament:     1 cal. .30 MG (Traverse 21 degrees, search 38 degrees)

Armor:        0.25 in. to 0.5 in.

Engine:       2 Ford Model T, 4 cyl.  Combined HP-45.

Speed:        8 MPH.   14.5 HP per Ton.

Transmission: Planetary - 2 speeds forward, 1 reverse.

Steering:

Cruising Radius:  34 miles

Slope Climbing:   25 degrees.

Suspension:   Leaf springs with rollers and bogies. Distributed unit spring.

Tracks:       Flat steel plates with grousers-Width 7 in.-Pitch 7 in.

Obstacle Ability:  20 in.

Spanning:     5 ft.

Ground Pressure:

Remarks:      Machine Gun had limited traverse.  Low and easily maneuvered. A fair accompanying tank, except for limited fire power, defective cooling and ventilation, cramped quarters and other minor faults. Produced by the Ford Motor Company.

# CHARACTERISTICS, U. S. TANKS

Name:    Mark I- 3 Man 1918- (1 Built)

Crew:    3.

General Arrangements: Driver left front, macine gunner right front, 37 mm
                      gun in center, engine and final drive in rear.

Weight:            7.5 Tons

Dimensions:    Length- 16 ft. 5 in.  Width 6 ft. 6 in.  Height - 7 ft. 9 in.

Clearance:

Fording:

Armament:    1-37 mm,   1 cal. .30 MG.

Armor:        0.37 in. to 0.5 inches.

Engine:      Hudson 6 cyl.  60hp water cooled.

Speed:       9 MPH.       8 HP per Ton.

Transmission: Planetary- one on each side.  2 speeds forward, 1 reverse.

Steering:

Cruising Radius:

Slope Climbing:

Suspension:  Leaf springs and pivoted bogies.

Tracks:      Pressed steel plates- Width 12 in.  Pitch 7 in.

Obstacle Ability:

Spanning:

Ground Pressure:

Remarks:     Center of Gravity was too far to the rear to negotiate obstacles
             satisfactorily.  Track adjustment method unsatisfactory because
             idlers could not be moved independently.  Produced by Ford Motor
             Company.

Name:    Mark VIII 1919   (100 built)

Crew:    11

General Arrangements: Crew compartment in front, engine compartment in rear,
                      driver in front of crew compartment.

Weight:               43.5 Tons. (fully equipped)

Dimensions: Length- 34 ft. 2½in.  Width- 12 ft. 5 in.  Height 10 ft. 2½ in.

Clearance:  20 3/4 in.

Fording:    2 ft.

Armament:   2  six pounders (2.24 in.) guns  and 5 cal. .30 MGS.

Armor:      0.236 in. to 0.63 in.

Engine:     Liberty 12 cylinder V-Type- 338 HP   Water Cooled.

Speed:      6.5 MPH     7.8 HP per Ton.

Transmission:  Planetary. 2 speeds forward, 1 reverse.

Steering:      Epicyclic

Cruising Radius:   50 miles.

Slope Climbing:    40 degrees

Suspension:        Rigid with rollers

Tracks:            Flat armor plate with grousers- Width 26½ in.
                   Pitch 11.15 in.

Obstacle Ability:  54 in.

Spanning:          16 ft.

Ground Pressure:   Ordnance figures for ground pressure -1 in. Penetration,
                   9.7 per square inch.    5 in penetration , 6.05 lbs.
                   per square inch.

Remarks:       Produced by Ordnance Department U.S.A.  6 pounder guns, the
               armor plate and various parts furnished by Great Britain.

## CHARACTERISTICS, U. S. TANKS

Name:   6 Ton  1917   ( 952 built )

Crew:   2

General Arrangements: Driver in front, gunner in center, engine and final
                      drive in rear.

Weight:          7.25 Tons.

Dimensions:   Length- 16 ft. 5 in.  Width 5 ft. 10½ in. Height- 7 ft.7 in.

Clearance:    16 3/16 inches.

Fording:      2 ft.

Armament:     1-37 mm gun, or 1 cal. .30 MG.

Armor:        0.25 in. to 0.6 in.

Engine:       Buda-4 cyl, 42 HP.  Water Cooled.

Speed:        5.5 mPH      5.8 HP per Ton.

Transmission: Sliding gear- 4 speeds forward, 1 reverse.

Steering:     Steering clutches and brake.

Cruising Radius:   30 miles.

Slope Climbing:    35 degrees.

Suspension:        Coil and leaf springs, and bogies and rollers

Tracks:            Flat steel plates with grousers- width 13 3/8 in
                   Pitch 9.84 in.

Obstacle Ability: 3 ft 8 in.

Spanning:         7 ft.

Ground Pressure:  6.9 lbs per square inch.

Remarks:

Name:     Pilot Model 6 Ton  M-1917  Al. (1 built)

Crew:     See note below

General Arrangements:

Weight:

Dimensions: Length 17 ft. 3½ in.  Width 7 ft. 10½ in.  Height 7 ft 7 in.

Clearance:

Fording:

Armament:

Armor:

Engine:   Franklyn 6 cylinder.  67 HP,air cooled.  Vertical draft.

Speed:    10.3 MPH.  9.2 HP per Ton .

Transmission: Same as 6- Ton Model 1917.  Case was reinforced.

Steering:

Cruising Radius:  50 miles.  29 gallons.

Slope Climbing:

Suspension:

Tracks:

Obstacle Ability:

Spanning:

Ground Pressure:

Remarks:  A six ton Model 1917 Tank was modified by removing the Buda engine
          with clutch radiator with fan and minor parts  by enlarging the
          engine compartment slightly,  and by installing a modified Franklyn,
          air cooled engine, complete with clutch, and with fans mounted on this
          tank of modified idlers which reduced the characteristic noise of the
          tank. Modified in 1929 by Engineering Department, Holabird Q.M.
          Depot.

-9-

## CHARACTERISTICS, U. S. TANKS

Name:  Six Ton, Model 1917 A1.  Modified 1930-1931 by the Ordnance Dept
       Total Production 7

Crew:  2

General Arrangements:  Same as 6 Ton Pilot Model

Weight:  7.1 Tons

Dimensions: 17 ft. 3½ in. Length.  Width 7 ft. 10½ in.  Height 7 ft. 7 in.

Clearance:

Fording:

Armament:

Armor:

Engine:  Franklyn 6 cylinder.  100 HP, air cooled, side draft.
         14.2 HP per Ton.

Speed:  9 MPH (governed)

Transmission:  Same as 6 Ton Tank (substantially)

Steering:          "   "   "   "   "              "

Cruising Radius:  50 miles, 29 gallons.           "

Slope Climbing:  Same as 6 Ton Tank              "

Suspension:        "     "   "b "     "            "

Tracks:            "       "   "   "     "        "

Obstacle Ability: "     "   "   "     "          "

Spanning:          "     "   "  "     "           "

Ground Pressure:  "     "   "  "     "           "

Remarks:  Substantially the same as the Pilot Model except that the engine
          and transmission were mounted upon a unit supporting - frame, and
          a more powerful engine was used. Due to the weakness of the old
          units still used,  the engine speed was governed down from
          3100 RPM to 2500 RPM.   The pilot model ,  later modified,
          constituted one of these seven tanks. Twelve volt ignition
          and batteries were installed,  the latter to be used with radio
          apparatus.

# CHARACTERISTICS, U. S. TANKS

**Name:** Medium A, M 1921 (1 built)
Produced 1921 by Ordnance Department.

**Crew:** 4

**General Arrangements:** Driver in front, gunners in center, engine and final drive in rear.

**Weight:** 23 Tons.

**Dimensions:** Length- 21 ft. 5 in. Width- 8 ft. Height 9 ft. 9 in.

**Clearance:** 17½ in.

**Fording:** 3 ft.

**Armament:** One 6 pounder gun ( 57 mmO -2.24 in.) and one cal. .30 MG in one mount in main turret; one cal..30 MG in upper turret.

**Armor:** 0.375 in to 1.0 in.

**Engine:** Murray and Tregurtha , (Marine), 6 cylinder. 250 HP (overhead valves) , governed to 170 HP, water cooled.
Later replaced by Packard, 8 cylinder engine, 200 BHP.

**Speed:** 10.1 MPH    7.4 HP per ton , governed.

**Transmission:** *Check p 160*

**Steering:** Epicyclic

**Cruising Radius:** 50 miles

**Slope Climbing:** 35 degrees

**Suspension:** Bogies, rollers and coil springs.

**Tracks:** Solid steel plates with grousers. Grousers were hollow and constituted oil reservoirs for lubrication of track pins.

**Obstacle Ability:** 26 in. Tree 12 in.

**Spanning:** 8 ft.

**Ground Pressure:** 10 pounds per square inch at 0 penetration

**Remarks:** The small upper turret, carrying one machine gun, revolved upon the larger turret as a base. A Liberty 338 HP engine was installed on this tank as an experiment and with it a maximum speed of 25 MPH was attained. A gear pump fuel system was used. A rotary water-expelling was provided and was driven from the transmission.

CHARACTERISTICS, U. S. TANKS

Name:     Medium, M 1922  (1 built)
          Produced 1922 by Ordnance Department

Crew:     4

General Arrangements: Driver in front; gunners in center; engine and final
                      drive in rear.

Weight:   25 Tons

Dimensions: Length - 26 ft. Width 9 ft. Height- 9 ft. 8½ in.

Clearance: 22 in.

Fording:   26 in.

Armament: One 6 pounder ( 57 mm-2.24 in.) gun and one cal. .30 MG in one mount
          in main turret. One cal. .30 in upper turret.

Armor:    0.375 in. to 1.0 in.

Engine:   Murray and Tregurtha, marine, 6 cyl., Maximum HP 250. Governed HP 170,
          forced water cooling ( same as  M 1921 )

Speed:    15.7 MPH.   6.8 HP per Ton.

Transmission: Bevel and epicyclic gear (planetary and sliding gear),  4 speeds
              forward and 1 reverse.  Pneumatic control of transmission and
              brakes.

Steering:

Cruising Radius:  Items not listed were in general similar to Medium Tank,
                  M 1921.

Slope Climbing:

Suspension:              *Check this item*

                  This suspension was found to be unsatisfactory.
Tracks:           Light wooden shoes within brackets, pivoted at the center and
                  held by a coil spring at each side.

Obstacle Ability:

Spanning:

Ground Pressure:

Remarks:   The track was higher in rear than in front and was generally
           unsatisfactory

## CHARACTERISTICS, U. S. TANKS

**Name:** Medium T 1   Recently renamed, T 1-E 1.  Has also been called
23 Ton, T 1.   Produced in 1925 by Ordnance Department.
Total production, 1.

**Crew:** 4

**General Arrangements:** Driver in front; gunners in center; engine and
final drive in rear.

**Weight:** 22 Tons

**Dimensions:** Length 21 ft. 6 in.  Width 8 ft.   Height 9 ft. 7$\frac{1}{2}$ in.

**Clearance:**

**Fording:** 2 ft.

**Armament:** One 6 pounder ( 57 mm-2.24 in.) gun and 1 cal .30 MG in one mount
in main turret, and one cal. .30 Mg in upper turret.

**Armor:** 0.375 in. to 1.0 in.

**Engine:** Special Packard V-type , 200 HP, forced water cooling.

**Speed:** 11.3 MPH  9.1 HP per Ton.

**Transmission:** Planetary and sliding gear, 4 speeds forward and 1 reverse.

**Steering:**

**Cruising Radius:** 50 miles
95 gallons

**Slope Climbing:** 35 degrees.

**Suspension:** Unit sprung
Bogies,rollers and coil springs.

**Tracks:** Forged steel skeleton type with grousers-width 18 in. pitch 8 1/8 in.

**Obstacle Ability:** 31 in vertical wall.   Tree , 12 in.

**Spanning:** 8 ft.

**Ground Pressure:** High.

**Remarks:** This tank has an unusually high ground pressure, it has not as great
HP per ton as is desirable, and it has a number of lesser faults.
In spite of all this , it is a good tank and is fairly well suited
to a definite tactical mission- that of the leading role.   A Liberty
338 HP engine has recently been installed in place of the special
Packard ( written 1933)

Name:     **MEDIUM T 2**
          Produced in 1930 by James Cunningham, Sons and Company. (Ordnance Design.   Total production 1.

Crew:     4

General Arrangements: Driver in left front, engine in right front, gunners in center;  ammunition space and final drive in rear.

Weight:   15 Tons.

Dimensions: Length 16 ft. Width 8 ft.  Height. 9 ft. 1 in.

Clearance:

Fording:  48 in.

Armament:  One 47 mm (1.85 in.) gun and one cal..50.MG in one mount in turret; one 37mm (1.46 in.) and one cal .30 MG in one mount in the hull.

Armor:    0.25 to 0.85 inches.

Engine:   Liberty V-12, 318 HP (modified), forced water cooling.  Compression low, resulting in reduced HP.

Speed:    25 MPH (governed to 20 MPH)

Transmission: Cotta sliding gear, 4 speeds forward and 1 reverse.

Steering:

Cruising Radius:  90 miles
                  94 gallons gas capacity.

Slope Climbing:   35 degrees.

Suspension:   Bogies, rollers and coil springs
              unit sprung.
              Front and rear rollers, which are slightly elevated
Tracks:   Cast steel skeleton type with long integral grousers.  Width 15 in. Pitch 5¼ in.

Obstacle Ability:   2 ft.

Spanning:   6 ft.

Ground Pressure:
              Gunners interfere with each other.   Guns mounted in the hull
              have limited traverse.  One cal .30 MG substituted in 1931
Remarks:      for one 37 mm gun and machine gun; one cal.30  AA gun
              added.  The steering brakes of this tank are operated through a
              vacuum booster.  An experimental gunner's seat is attached to
              the gun cradle, and the weight of the receiver, the gunner and
              gunner's seat is counterbalanced by counterweights(over 600lbs.)
              mounted in front of the gun mount trunnion pins.   A Sperry
              electric-driven gyroscopic direction indicator has been installed.

# CHARACTERISTICS, U. S. TANKS

Name: ONE MAN EXPERIMENTAL TANK
Track Developement Chassis, T 1   Produced 1928 by James Cunningham,
Sons and Company.  (Ordnance design) Total production 1

Crew:  1.

General Arrangements: Transmission in front, engine in center; man in rear.
Man straddles  rear part of engine .

Weight: 1.5 Tons.

Dimensions: Length 8 ft. 7 in.  Width 4 ft. 9 in. Height. 5 ft. 1½ in.

Clearance:

Fording:

Armament:  One  cal. .30 machine gun.

Armor:  0.125 in.

Engine: Ford Model A, 4 cylinder , 42 HP, water cooled.

Speed: 19.5 MPH.   28 HP per Ton.

Transmission: Sliding gear, 3 speeds forward, i reverse.

Steering:

Cruising Radius:

Slope Climbing:

Suspension: Rear wheels slightly sprung,(coil springs). Unsprung front wheels
drive; wheels of aluminum;  solid rubber tires.

Tracks: Each track includes two flexible steel bands 4½ inches wide, lined
with commercial belting; steel grousers outside, guiding lugs on
inner surface; Total track width 10 inches.

Obstacle Ability:

Spanning:

Ground Pressure:

Remarks:    The experimental development of tracks eas an impo rtant purpose
of this construction.

## CHARACTERISTICS, U. S. TANKS

**Name:** CHRISTIE M 1919
Produced in 1919 by the Front Drive Motor Company. Total Production 1.

**Crew:** 3

**General Arrangements:** Driver in front, gunners in center, engine and final drive in rear.

**Weight:** 13.5 Tons

**Dimensions:** Length 18. ft. 2 in. Width 8 ft. 6 in. Height 9 ft.

**Clearance:**

**Fording:**

**Armament:** One six pounder (57mm-2.24 in.) gun in main turret and one cal. .30 MG in upper turret.

**Armor:** 0.25 to 1.0 in.

**Engine:** Christie, 6 cylinder, 120 HP, water cooled.

**Speed:**

**Transmission:** Sliding gear, 4 speeds forward and 1 reverse.

**Steering:**

**Cruising Radius:** 35 miles on tracks, 75 miles on wheels. Fuel capacity 59 gal.

**Slope Climbing:**

**Suspension:** Rubber tired wheels, center wheels only sprung.

**Tracks:** Removable; flat steel plates, 15 in wide; pitch 9 3/4 in.

**Obstacle Ability:**

**Spanning:**

**Ground Pressure:**

**Remarks:** Tracks carried above the wheels when driving on wheels. Small pyramidal lugs on inside of plates fro driving and guiding tracks. Center wheels raised when running on wheels. 15 minutes to change from wheels to tracks or vice versa.

## CHARACTERISTICS, U. S. TANKS

**Name:** CHRISTIE M 1921
Rebuilt from the 1919 tank in 1921 by the Front Drive Motor Company
Total production 1.

**Crew:** 4

**General Arrangements:** Gunners in front; Commander and driver in center
(driver at left ); engine and final drive in rear.

**Weight:** 14 Tons

**Dimensions:** Length 18 ft. 2 in. Width 8 ft. 6 in. Height 7 ft. 1 in.

**Clearance:**

**Fording:**

**Armament:** One 6 pounder (57 mm-2.24in) gun in front and one cal. .30 MG
on each side.

**Armor:** 0.25 to 0.75 in.

**Engine:** Christie 6 cylinder, 120 HP, forced water cooling. Mounted laterly
Horse Power per ton 8.6

**Speed:** 7 MPH on tracks; 14 MPH on wheels.

**Transmission:** Sliding gear, 4 speeds forward, 4 speeds reverse; a complete
transmission on each side.

**Steering:**

**Cruising Radius:** 60 miles on tracks, 100 miles on wheels. Fuel capacity
67 gallons.

**Slope Climbing:** 40 degrees.

**Suspension:** Wheels with double rubber tires; front wheels sprung with
coil springs, center wheels on pivoted bogies.

**Tracks:** Removable; flat steel plates with grousers and driving lugs;
width 15 in., pitch 9 3/4 in.

**Obstacle Ability:** Trench $7\frac{1}{2}$ ft.

**Spanning:** "　" "

**Ground Pressure:**

**Remarks:-**
Drive wheels unsprung; crew compartment small; maneuverability poor.

# CHARACTERISTICS, U. S. TANKS

**Name:** CHRISTIE CHASSIS, M 1928
Produced in 1928 by U.S. Wheel Track Layer Corporation.  1 Built.

**Crew:** Undetermined.

**General Arrangements:** Crew compartment in front; driver in left rear part
of crew compartment; engine and final drive in rear.

**Weight:** 8.6 Tons

**Dimensions:** Length 17 ft.; width 7 ft.; Height 6 ft.

**Clearance:**

**Fording:** 5 ft.

**Armament:** Undetermined

**Armor:** 0.5 in.

**Engine:** Liberty,12 cylinder, V-type, 338 HP, forced water cooling.

**Speed:** 42.5 MPH on tracks;  70 MPH on wheels.

**Transmission:** Sliding gear, 4 speeds forward, one reverse,

**Steering:**

**Cruising Radius:** 75 miles on tracks.  115 miles on wheels. Fuel capacity
35 gallons.

**Slope Climbing:** 37 degrees

**Suspension:** Essentially-Four large weight bearing wheels on each side, each with
dual rubber tires and mounted upon a pivoted arm upon which bears
a long coil spring. The liberal compression amplitude gives each of
**Tracks:** these wheels an independent maximum vertical movement of about 14 in.
Forged steel plates with U-shaped driving lugs attached to each alternate
plate. Width 10 in.  Pitch 10 in.
**Obstacle Ability:** Vertical 28 in.

**Spanning:** Trench 7 ft.

**Ground Pressure:**

**Remarks:** This was the forerunner of the 1931 tank, and although lighter in
weight was similar as a vehicle to the later tank in all essential
features.

18

# CHARACTERISTICS, U. S. TANKS

Name:  Convertible Medium Tank, T-3  (CHRISTIE, M 1931)
        Produced in 1931 by the U.S. Wheel Track Layer Corporation.  Total
        Production 7.

Crew:  2

General Arrangements:  Driver in front; gunner in center; engine and final
                        Drive in rear

Weight:  10½ Tons

Dimensions:
| Length | Width | Height |
|---|---|---|
| 17 ft. 10 in. | 7 ft. 4 in. | 7 ft. 3 in. |

( The height varies slightly with the adjustment of the suspension springs.)

Clearance:  14 in.

Fording:  4 ft.  ( Howie says "3½ ft.")

Armament:  One 37 mm (1.46 in.) gun and one cal. .30 MG in dual mount.

Armor:  0.25 to 0.625 in. exclusive of 0.188 in. inner hull of nickle
        steel. (Howie says "Boilerplate")

Engine:  Liberty V-12, 338 HP.  Water cooled.

Speed:  Wheels 70 MPH Tracks 45 MPH.   30.7 HP per Ton.

Transmission:  Selective sliding
                4 speeds forwards,
                1 reverse.

Steering:  Wheels-rack & pinion
            Track-steering clutches.

Cruising Radius: Wheels 200-
                  Track 100 miles.

Slope Climbing:  35 degrees.

Suspension:  Four large weight-bearing wheels on each side, each with dual
              rubber tires and mounted upon a pivoted arm upon which bears a
              long adjustable coil spring.  The liberal compression amplitude

Tracks:  gives each of these wheels an independent vertical movement of
          about 14 in.
          Tracks-Forged steel plates, each alternate plate having a

Obstacle Ability:  driving lug integral therewith; width 10½ in. pitch 10 in.

                    3 ft.

Spanning:          7 ft.

Ground Pressure:   8.3 lbs per sq. in.

Remarks:  Six of these seven tanks have chain drive from sprocket to rear
          road wheel when on wheels; the other has gear drive instead.  Thirty
          minutes is required to change from tracks to wheels and vice versa.
          Two additional chassis of this type were purchased by Russia.  In
          February, 1931,, one of these tanks (U.S. Tanks) made a cross country
          run of 141 miles at an average speed of 21.1 mph with no mechanical
          difficulties

## CHARACTERISTICS, U. S. TANKS

**Name:** CHRISTIE LIGHT TANK, M 1932
Produced in 1932 by U.S. Wheel Track Layer Corporation. Total
Production 1.

**Crew:** 3.

**General Arrangements:** Cannon in front ; crew in front center; engine and final
drive in rear.

**Weight:** About 5 Tons.

**Dimensions:** Length 20 ft. Width. 7 ft. Height 5 ft. 8 in. without turret.

**Clearance:**

**Fording:**

**Armament:** Undetermined ( can carry 1 cannon and one or more MGS ).

**Armor:** 0.375 to 0.5 in. (Thicker armor may be installed.)

**Engine:** Hispano-Suiza V-type 12 cylinder 750 HP water cooled

**Speed:** 120 MPH on wheels, 60 MPH on tracks

**~~Transmission~~** Similar to 1931 model but with a maximum vertical movement of
**Suspension:** 24 in.; wheels of duraluminum with pneumatic wheels.

**Steering:**

**Cruising Radius:** 89 gal. capacity

**Slope Climbing:**

**~~Suspension~~:**
**Transmission:** Sliding gear 3 speeds forward and one reverse; has a power
take off for operating proposed flying propeller.

**Tracks:** Steel plates; width 11 in; pitch 7 in; Track pins 3/8 in diameter.

**Obstacle Ability:** Can jump 12 foot ditch or trench.

**Spanning:**

**~~Ground Pressure~~:** Very light construction throughout. In this design it was
contemplated that this vehicle could be carried up by a
special airplane carrier and later released close to the
ground. Cross-flow horizontal engines above the engine.
**Remarks:**

## CHARACTERISTICS, U. S. TANKS

Name:   LIGHT TANK , T 1
         Produced in 1927 by James Cunningham , Sons and Company.
         (Ordnance Design) Total production 1.

Crew:  2

General Arrangements: Engine in front;  driver in center; gunner and
                         final drive in rear.

Weight:  7.5 Tons.

Dimensions:  Length, 12 ft. 6 inches. Width, 5 ft. $10\frac{1}{2}$ in.  Height 7 ft. $1\frac{1}{2}$ in.

Clearance:

Fording:  20 inches

Armament:  One 37 mm. gun and one cal. .30 MG in dual mount.

Armor:    0.25 to 0.375 inches.

Engine:  Cunningham 8 cylinder V-type, 105 HP, Water cooled .

Speed:  20 MPH , 14 HP per Ton.

Transmission: Cotta sliding gear,
           3 speeds forward and 1 reverse.

Steering:

Cruising Radius: 65 miles.

Slope Climbing: 30 degrees

Suspension: Unsprung rollers and bogies.  Bogies connected to a swing link,
          the latter being pivoted to the track frame.

Tracks: Cast steel skeleton type with grousers. Width 12 inches. Pitch 6.5 in.

Obstacle Ability: 20 in.

Spanning:  six feet.

Ground Pressure:

Remarks:  The series of light tanks , of which this was the first, embodied
         numerous improvements in design over earlier U.S. tanks.  The tanks
         were not, however, deemed satisfactory, due to the general arrange-
         ment and the inability of the suspension to cope adequately with
         vibration and shocks.  This particular tank was later converted into
         a cargo carrier, and, from that, into a motorized reel carrier for the
         artillery.

# CHARACTERISTICS, U. S. TANKS

Name: Light Tank T 1 E 1
      Produced in 1928 by James Cunningham, Sons and Company
      (Ordnance Design) Total produced, 4.

Crew: 2

General Arrangements: This tank differed only slightly from the T 1. The Projection of the body beyond the front extremities of the tracks was eliminated. The fule tanks were placed above the tracks. The air circulation was altered somewhat.

Weight: 15515 lbs.

Dimensions: Length 152½ inches; width 70½ inches, Height 85 5/8 inches.
              12ft 8½ in.          5 ft. 10½ in.      7 ft. 1 5/8 in.

Clearance: 14 inches

Fording: 19½ inches.

Armament: One 37 mm gun and one cal. .30 MG.

Armor: ⅛ to 3/8 inches.

Engine: Cunningham V-8

Speed: 20 MPH

Transmission: Cotta

Steering: Clutch Brake

Cruising Radius: 1.49 miles per gallon, 50 gallon capacity. 100 miles.

Slope Climbing: 45 degree slope.

Suspension: Link on rollers

Tracks: Cast steel open shoe, width 12 in. Pitch 6½ in.
      (According to "Fighting Tanks since 1916"-The skeleton track picked up barbed wire thereby stalling the tank)

Obstacle Ability:

Spanning:

Ground Pressure:

Remarks: Dates of tests-August 1926 to January 1930. Designed in 1927 by the Ordnance Department and 4 vehicles built by James Cunningham Sons and Co.
      One vehicle was tested at the proving ground in 1928 and proved the best tank produced by the Ordnance Department to that time. Numerous minor modifications were recommended after which the vehicle was to be considered suitable for standardization. Also recommended a redesign to incorporate the modifications found necessary by the proving ground tests.

## CHARACTERISTICS, U. S. TANKS

Name:     Light Tank , T1 E2
          Produced in 1929 by James Cunningham, Sons and Company.
          Total Produced, 1.

Crew:   2

General Arrangements:  Same as T1

Weight:   8.9 Tons

Dimensions: Length, 12 ft. 8½ in. Width 6 ft. 2 in. Height 7 ft 6½ in.

Clearance:

Fording: 20 in.

Armament: One 37 mm semi-automatic and one cal..30MG in dual mount.

Armor:  0.25 to 0.625 inches.

Engine:  Cunningham 8 cyl. V-Type, 132 HP,
          Water cooled.

Speed: 16 MPH, 14.8 HP per Ton.

Transmission: Same as T1 (modified)

Steering:

Cruising Radius:   75 miles.

Slope Climbing: 27 degrees

Suspension:  Same type as T1

Tracks:   Same as T1 Width 13 in. Pitch 6.75 in.

Obstacle Ability: 22 inches.

Spanning:   6 ft.

Ground Pressure: Minor defects in T1 E1 were corrected. Armor was increased.
               Engine HP. was increased. (Ordnance Design)

Remarks:

## CHARACTERISTICS, U. S. TANKS

Light Tank , T1E3

**Name:** T1 E3  This was a modification of one of the T1E1 Tanks  effected by the Ordnance Department in 1930.  Total Production 1.

**Crew:** 2

**General Arrangements:** Same as T1E1

**Weight:** 8.9 Tons  (Fighting Tanks since 1916 gives 8.5Tons)

**Dimensions:** Practically the same as T1E1

**Clearance:** 14 in.

**Fording:** 20 in.

**Armament:** One 37 mm. semi-automatic, 2000 f.s. and one cal. .30 MG.

**Armor:** Front .625, sides .5 in.  Top .25 in.   Bottom .25 in.

**Engine:** Same as T1E2

**Speed:** 20 mph.  15.6 HP per Ton.

**Transmission:** Same as T1E2

**Steering:**

**Cruising Radius:** 75 miles

**Slope Climbing:** 35 degrees

**Suspension:** Unit sprung.  Medium T2 type of rollers with double row of ball bearings installed on the three rear bogies. Two track supporting rollers added. (Fighting Tanks Since 1916,Has: Rollers, bogies, vertical coil springs within hydraulic shock absorbers. The shock absorbing action acts in only one direction.

**Tracks:** Same as T1E1.

**Obstacle Ability:** 22 in.

**Spanning:** 6 ft.

**Ground Pressure:**

**Remarks:** The improved suspension materially improved the riding qualities This was the only important modification.  A supplementary floor was installed in the gunner's compartment flush with the top of the transmission.

Name: Light Tank T1-E4
Produced in 1932 by the Ordnance Department Total Production 1

Crew: 4

General Arrangements: Driver, Transmission and final drive in front,
gunner in center, engine in rear.

Weight: 8.6 Tons

Dimensions: Length 15.5 ft. Width 7 ft. 2 3/4 in Height. 6 ft. 6 3/4 in.

Clearance:

Fording:

Armament: Same as T1E3

Armor: 0.25 to 0.625 in.

Engine: Cunningham 8 cylinder V-type, 140 HP. Water Cooled.

Speed: 20 MPH.

Transmission: Cotta type sliding gear, 3 speeds forward, 1 reverse.

Steering:

Cruising Radius:

Slope Climbing: 30 degrees.

Suspension: Pivoted semi-elyptical springs and Bogies. Rollers with dual
solid rubber tires.

Tracks: Forged steel plates, mostly solid, giving surface for rollers, but open
at edges for double sprocket teeth. No grousers. Width 13¼ in.
Pitch 4 in.
Obstacle Ability:

Spanning: 7 ft.

Ground Pressure:

Remarks: This tank is a modification of the T1E1 design. The engine, power
train and final drive are reversed, thus placing the engine in rear
and the final drive in front. There are adjustable air louvres in
the fire screen. Produced by the Ordnance Department.

CHARACTERISTICS, U. S. TANKS

Name: Light Tank T1E5 (1 built)

Crew: 2

General Arrangements: Crew in rear of tank

Weight: 15,800 lbs.

Dimensions: Length 152½ in. Width 70½ in. Height 85 5/8 in.
            12 ft 8½ in.     5 ft 10½ in.     7 ft. 1 5/8 in.
            Height of pintle above ground 29 in.
Clearance: 14 in.

Fording: 10½ in. safe depth.

Armament: 1 37 mm gun    1   cal. . 30 MG

Armor: ¼ to 3/8 in.

Engine: Cunningham V-8 .    17.7 HP per Ton

Speed: 19.64 MPH constant reduction at 3000 RPM

Transmission: Cotta 3 speeds forward 1 reverse.

Steering: Controlled differential

Cruising Radius: Not stated. Gasoline capacity 50 gallons.

Slope Climbing: Not stated.

Suspension: Solid track on rollers. Link type, cast steel shoe

Tracks: Cast steel shoe. Width 12 in. Pitch 6½ in.

Obstacle Ability: Not stated.

Spanning: Not stated.

Ground Pressure:

Remarks: Dates of tests- October to November 1932. Light Tank T1E1 No. 4 was
modified to incorporate a controlled differential steering unit,
supplied by the Cleveland Tractor Company, in place of the Clutch
Brake steering system. Cunningham engine replaced with another
Cunningham engine of the same type, but modified to develop more
power.   Test showed superiority of the controlled differential
steering in Light Tank T1E6 and in the Combat Car T4. The controlled
differential was also considered with a view of making it standard for all
tracklaying vehicles with speeds in excess of 6 miles per hour.

CHARACTERISTICS, U. S. TANKS

Name: LIGHT TANK, T1 E6  (1 built)

Crew: 3

General Arrangements:

Weight: 19,900

Dimensions:     Length 185 in.   Width 86 3/4 in. Height 78 3/4 in.
                     15 ft. 5 in.    7 ft 2 3/4 in.    6 ft. 6 3/4 in.
                Height of pintle above ground 16 3/4 in.
Clearance:      10 3/4 inches.

Fording:        Not stated

Armament:       One 37 mm semi-Automatic and 1 cal. .30 MG.

Armor:          1/4 to 5/8 inches.

Engine:         American La France Overhead Valves.  V-12
                Compression ratio -5.16

Speed:          Constant reduction 19.64.   High at 2800 rpm.

Transmission:  Cotta.

Steering:      Clutch and brake.

Cruising Radius: Not stated.  Gas capacity, 50 gallons.

Slope Climbing:    Not stated.

Suspension:       Leaf Spring articulating bogie on steering clutch.

Tracks:           Width 23 in.  Pitch 4 in.   Tread 68 in.

Obstacle Ability: Not stated.

Spanning:     Not stated.

Ground Pressure:   Zero penetration 6/ .75

Remarks:     This is the Light Tank T1 E4 modified to incorporate the 244 HP
             American La France V-12 cylinder in place of the Cunningham engine
             of the T1 E4.  Engine performs very satisfactorily, but is inaccessible
             due to crowded installation.  Transmission runs hot as in T1 E4.  The
             only advantage of the front sprocket drive is to help ballance the
             heavy engine in the rear and this move the center of gravity of the
             tank forward.  Track very satisfactory.  Originally light tank
             T1 E1 and later Light Tank T1 E4 before the present designation.

# CHARACTERISTICS, U. S. TANKS

Name: Medium Tank T1E1

Crew:     4

General Arrangements:

Weight:   44500 lbs.   about 22.25 Tons

Dimensions:   Length 258 inches  Width 96 inches  Height 112½ inches
                 21 ft. 6 in.       8 ft.          9 ft 4½ in.

Clearance:   Not stated

Fording:        "       "

Armament:    One 6 pounder gun and 2 cal. .30 mgs.

Armor:      ¼ to 1 inch.

Engine:      Liberty V-12

Speed:      Speed not stated

Transmission: Bevel gear and epicyclic gear, forged steel open shoe

Steering:    Epicyclic.

Cruising Radius:  0.7 miles per gallon.  95 gal. cap.

Slope Climbing:   not stated.

Suspension:      Coil springs

Tracks:      Width 18 inches.  Pitch 8½ inches.

Obstacle Ability:   Not stated.

Spanning:        "       "

Ground Pressure:     "       "

Remarks:    Date tested-April 1932.   This is the Medium Tank T1 modified
            by installing a Liberty Engine in place of the Packard engine.
            Reserve power is considered adequate and Generality of the tank
            good. Total produced 1.

Name:   LIGHT TANK T2 (M2) 1934.

Crew:   4

General Arrangements: Driver and one gunner in front, Engine in rear.  Two
                     guns in turrets.

Weight:  12705 Tons without guns, ammunition, gas and crew.

Dimensions:   Length 160½ inches. Width 93½ inches  Height  81 inches
              13 ft. 4½ in.        7 ft. 9½ in.        6 ft. 9 in.

Clearance:   13½ inches

Fording:     15 inches, safe.

Armament:    Two cal..30 MGs  and one cal. .50 Mg.

Armor:       5/8 inches turret and front.  3/8 inches side. ¼ inch Engine
             Hood, rear and bottom.

Engine:      Continental radial, 7 cylinder, type R670.  Cooled by air blower
             type, special fan

Speed:       45 miles per hour.

Transmission:  Special Spicer Mfg. Co. Spur gear final drive.

Steering:      Controlled differential

Cruising Radius:   100 miles

Slope Climbing;    5 feet 2 inches.

Suspension:        Double leaf spring articulating bogie.

Tracks:            Rubber jointed integral grousers.

Obstacle Ability:

Spanning:          5 feet 2 inches.

Ground Pressure:   13.

Remarks:   Dates tested-April -May 1934.  This vehicle was designed by the
           Ordnance Department and the Pilot Vehicle built at the Rock Island
           Arsenal in 1934.  It is full track laying (non-convertible) with
           a suspension system substantially the same as the Light Tank T1E6,
           and the Vickers-Armstrong 6-Ton British Tank.  The essentials of the
           hull and power plant are identical to Combat Car T-5 except for
           slightly heavier armor on the tank.  Pilot Vehicles given a brief
           test at Aberdeen Proving and it was found that as at present con-
           structed it is unable to operate mechanically as intended for more
           than a brief period.  Some major defects include the too weak

construction of the bogie suspension system, inaccessibility of some of the major
units of the power train and their accessories for proper inspection and servicing,
the doubtful merit of rubber bushings in tracks for high speed vehicles because of
the great lateral flexibility of the track permitted by such bushings.    Vehicle
returned to Rock Island Arsenal for installation of new suspension system.  Manufactured by Rock Island Arsenal, Ordnance Department.

# CHARACTERISTICS, U. S. TANKS

Name:   Light Tank M2A1 (formerly, T2E1)

Crew:   4

General Arrangements: Driver and one gunner in front.  One gun in turret,
Engine in rear of tank.

Weight:   14635, full of gas with driver, less guns and ammunition.

Dimensions: Length-161¼ inches   Width-88½ inches   Height- 81 inches
            13 ft. 5⅜in.            7 ft. 4½ in.         6 ft. 9 inches.

Clearance:  13¼ inches. Height of pintle above ground-front, 25 in. Rear, 20 in.

Fording:

Armament:  One cal. .30 Mg.   One cal. .30 and one cal. .50MG in turret.

Armor:    Turret and frontal area 5/8 in.  Sides 3/8 in.  Engine Hood and
          rear ¼ in.

Engine:   Continental Radial 7 cylinder Type R670

Speed:    45 miles per hour.

Transmission: Special Spicer.

Steering:   Controlled Differential

Cruising Radius:  100 miles

Slope Climbing:   Same as T2

Suspension:      Volute Spring and bogies, 20 X 6 X 16.  Industrial tires
                 on bogies

Tracks:        Rubber Block, T16 detachable

Obstacle Ability:  Same as T2

Spanning:        Same as T2

Ground Pressure:  Not stated.

Remarks: Date of tests-October 1934.  The vehicle tested at Aberdeen Proving
Ground is the Pilot Light Tank T2 after modification at Rock Island
Arsenal, the chief item of modification being the substitution of a
volute spring type suspension similar to that on the Combat Car T5
for the leaf spring articulating bogie type, originally on the Light
Tank, T2.  The vehicle is now similar to the Combat car T5, differing
only in that it has a single turret and heavier armor plate.  Nine additional vehicles of this type of real armor are under manufacture.  They
are to be equipped with SCR 210 Radio sets.  This vehicle has recently
been standardized and given the name, "LIGHT TANK M2A1"

CHARACTERISTICS, U. S. TANKS

Name: MEDIUM TANK T3E2 (1934)    Total Produced  5.

Crew:  4

General Arrangements: Driver and gunner in front, 2 gunners in turret.

Weight: 28200 lbs,14.1 Tons

Dimensions:  Length 225 inches Width  8 feet    Height  92 inches
                        18 ft 9 in.        96 in.              7 ft. 8 in.

Clearance:  14 in.  Height of pintle above ground 16 in.

Fording:   Not stated

Armament: 5 cal.30  Mgs.  One 37 mm gun.

Armor:   Crew compartment ⅛ inch, top ¼ inch.  Elsewhere 3/8 inch.

Engine:  Curtis 12 cylinder type TD 12 DE.

Speed:   35 MPH on tracks.  57.6 MPH on wheels

Transmission:  Selective sliding 4 speeds forward and 1 reverse.
               Final drive chain.

Steering:    Clutch Brake.

Cruising Radius: 85 gal. capacity/  Tracks 1.0 miles per gallon.
                                    Wheels 2.0 miles per gallon.
                 Turning radius 28 feet left.  33 feet right.
Slope Climbing: 9 feet. Vertical wall 3 feet 6 inches.

Suspension:    Individually sprung wheels.

Tracks:        Forged steel plates.  Width 12 in.  Pitch 5 in.

Obstacle Ability:   35 degrees

Spanning:   9 feet.

Ground Pressure:  1 inch 8.3
                  Dates tested-May 1934 to October 1935.  This vehicle was built
                  by the American LaFrance Corporation of Elmira, N.Y. in 1933-1934.
Remarks:          Five vehicles were built at this time.  The vehicle is similar to the
                  Medium Tank T3 (Christie).  It is a complete redesign and not a
                  modification as the designation T3E2 might indicate.  The vehicle
                  is convertible (wheels or tracks) and embodies the individually
                  sprung wheel type of track suspension.  It is powered by a Curtis
                  D-12 water cooled Airplane engine, developing 435 brake horse
                  power.  The acceptance tests of all five vehicles were made at
                  Aberdeen Proving Ground in the spring of 1934.  One vehicle was

delivered to the Proving Ground for a complete proof test..

The proof test showed the performance characteristics to be generally very good, but that the durability and mechanical reliability are very unsatisfactory. The outstanding desirable features are the reliable engine of ample power, good riding qualities, due to the suspension system. General design provides good appearance and silhouette and low center of gravity, and a good track. The crew quarters are safe and comfortable and the turret is easily rotated.

The outstanding defects are: weak transmission and final drive systems; very unsatisfactory steering, due to the use of the clutch brake system of steering; general inaccessibility of working parts; excess armement in turret

Note ( It may be well to question this item of excess item/ armement in turret due to recent battlefield experiences in Spain and elsewhere).

LIGHT TANK M2A2 (Formerly T2E2)

This vehicle differs from the Light Tank M2A1 (T2E1) only in that it has two turrets instead of the single turret. Nine vehicles of this type are being produced with F.Y. 1935 funds, but the total number being produced applicable to Infantry is 128, of which 21 are for the National Guard. One hundred ad two (102) ofthese are to be equipped with radio sets, SCR 210, and 26 with SCR sets 193. These vehicles have recently been standardized and given the designation,"TANK, LIGHT, M2A2." Total production completed or under manufacture to date-128 (from Ordnance Digest, July 1935).

Light Tank M2 A3   (T2E3)

This vehicle is identicle with the light tanks T2E1 and T2E2  (M2A1, M2A2) except that the turrets are replaced by a Barbette Superstructure of a type decided upon by the Infantry Board as a result oftheir tests of the Combat Car T5E1 at Fort Benning.   It is plahned to produce six vehicles of this type( Ordnance Digest, July 1935).

Name:  Medium Tank T4 -1936

Crew:   4

General Arrangements:  Driver and gunner in front.  2 gunners in turret
Engine compartment in rear.

Weight:    32000 lbs.   16 Tons.

Dimensions: Length 16 ft. 1 in.   Height 7 ft. 3 3/8 in.  Width 8 ft. 1 3/4 in.

Clearance: 15 inches.

Fording:    3 feet.

Armament:  1 cal .50 and two cal. 30 mgs.

Armor:    Front 5/8 inch  Turret 5/8 in.  Sides ½ inch.  Rear ½ inch
Bottom ½ inch.

Engine:   Continental Radial 257 HP at 2400 Rev.

Speed:   Wheels 38 mph.   Tracks 23.5 mph.

Transmission: 4 speeds forward and 1 reverse.

Steering:  R & P- C & L Controlled Differential.

Cruising Radius:  Wheels 90 miles.   Track 45 miles. 41½ Gal cap.

Slope Climbing:  35 degrees, vertical wall 2 feet.

Suspension: Lever, individually sprung.  Vacuum Brakes & Mechanical on front
and rear wheels.

Tracks:    Width 14 inches  Pitch 4.75 inch.  Weight of track 1224 lbs.
96 links, 12½ lbs per link.  Final drive wheels and track enclosed .
Chain drive, sprocket and track change, track to wheels fifteen to
twenty minutes.

Obstacle Ability:

Spanning:

Ground Pressure:  9.9 at 1 inch.

Remarks:   This vehicle is the same in general design as the Combat Car
T4E1  but with Infantry armor protection of real armor.  The sides
and front of the hull have been modified slightly.  In order to
take care of the increased weight the capacity of the suspension
mechanism has been increased by the use of 6 inch diameter springs.
Five inch tires and the wheel arms and bearings strengthened
accordingly.  These vehicle have single turrets.  Since the
vehicle has little superiority in offensive or defensive

Medium Tank T4,1936  (Continued)

characteristics over the light tank T2 and costs almost twice as much
the standardization of this tank is not favorably considered by the office
of the Adjutant General.  ~~This tank is the same as the Medium~~

## MEDIUM TANK T4E1

This tank is the same as the Medium Tank T4; differing only in that it has
a barbette superstructure in lieu of turret.
Total number under production 3.
This tank has been recommended for standardization.
The standardization of this vehicle is not favorably considered by the
Adjutant General's Office.

## CHARACTERISTICS, U. S. TANKS

Name:   LIGHT TANK T3  (Ford)   *1936*

Crew:  2

General Arrangements:  Turning Radius 28 ft. 1 in.

Weight:   7000 pounds

Dimensions:   Length 135 inches  Width 81½ inches   Height   54 in.
              11 ft. 3 in.       6 ft. 9½ in.              4 ft. 6 in.

Clearance:       14 in. Height of pintle above ground 21 inches.

Fording: 28 inches.

Armament:  One cal. .30 Mg.

Armor: 3/16 inch bottom.  Top and rear ¼ inch.   Sides 3/8 inch
       Front pilot aluminum plate.

Engine: Ford V-8 type  Water cooled, 8 cylinder, Compression ratio, 5.3 to 1.

Speed: Constant reduction 5.34 at speed 3600 rpm.

Transmission:  Brown Lipe 2341.  4 speeds forward . 1 reverse.  Final drive
               spur gears single plate clutch.

Steering:      Controlled differential.

Cruising Radius:   4 miles per gallon, Gas capacity 30 gallons.

Slope Climbing:

Suspension:   Volute spring bogie

Tracks:       Rubber blocks.  Width 8½ inches.  Pitch 5 inches.

Obstacle Ability:

Spanning:     4 feet 6 inches.

Ground Pressure:  Not stated.

Remarks:   The pilot vehicle was manufactured at Rock Island Arsenal and is now
           undergoing tests at Aberdeen Proving Ground.  The suspension
           system is the volute spring type with articulating bogies.  The
           tracks are rubber blocks similar to the T16 series tracks used on
           the Light Tank T2E1.  Further comments on this vehicle are withheld
           pending completion of tests at Aberdeen Proving Ground.